LOVE. HERITAGE. WISDOM

LETTERS TO MY DAUGHTER

MEMORIES. LEGACY. GUIDANCE.

THIS BOOK
BELONGS TO:

MY DAUGHTER

In the words of Stephanie Lahart:

You are like an excellent cut diamond that shines brightly from within. You are admired by many, including me! You are joy, love, peace, and excellence. You are beautifully made.

With love always,

THE CON TENT

OUR FAMILY

Family Tree

Ancestral Origins

Notable Ancestors

SOME

Exciting Facts About You

Your First Words

Your first friend/friends

Your Love Language

Your Happy Place
(What excites you)

Your first book

Your first school

YOUR SIGNS

NAME &
SMALL BABY PHOTO

DATE, TIME,
AND PLACE OF BIRTH

ZODIAC

MOON AND SUN SIGNS

RISING SIGN

A FEW WORDS TO LIVE BY

- Keep a positive mindset; it attracts positive experiences.
- Prioritize your emotional, mental, and physical well-being.
- Safeguard your time and energy.
- Remain receptive to fresh ideas and viewpoints.
- Evaluate suggestions at all times.
- Exercise sound judgment in decision-making.
- Demonstrate a combination of kindness, wisdom, and love.
- “The only enduring beauty is the beauty of the heart.” - Rumi
- Don't forget to smile.

LESSONS FROM LIFE'S JOURNEY

Dear daughter, here are a few stories and experiences from my life's journey, each with its own lesson. Some will make you smile, others might bring tears, and a few could make you cringe. I share them with the hope that these lessons will help guide you on your own path.

"Our stories make us who we are. And each story has its own purpose and its own reward. Each story rings true and each story is worthy of the ages. There is no such thing as an insignificant life."

— *Laurence Overmire*

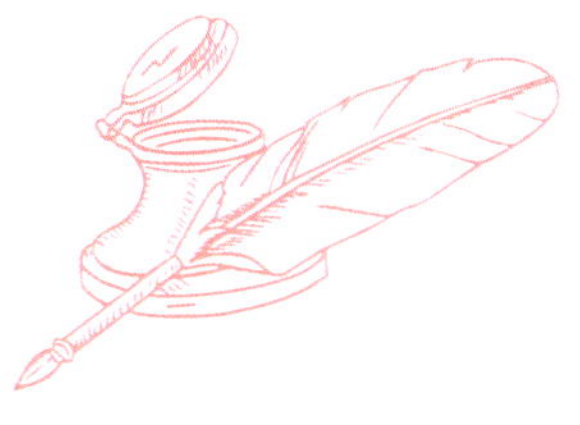

“A GRATEFUL

PARENT

RAISES A

GRATEFUL

CHILD”

— *inspired by Kristen Welch*

Timeless Wisdom

Dear daughter, Confucius once said, 'Three ways lead to wisdom: reflection, the noblest; imitation, the easiest; and experience, the bitterest.' I share the wisdom I have gained through my life experiences. May you find value in them and revisit them often.

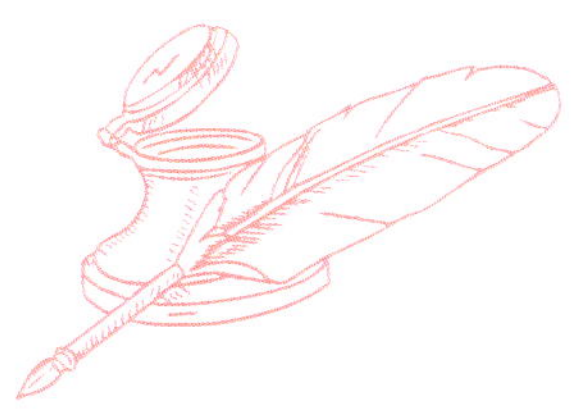

"TRAIN YOUR BRAIN TODAY... DON'T WAIT FOR LIFE TO BE THE TEACHER!"

— *Hamadene Aziz*

HERE'S TO A BRIGHT TOMORROW.

Dear daughter, as you pursue your goals and dreams, know that you are always supported and loved. Here are affirmations and encouraging messages to guide you on your journey to your highest good.

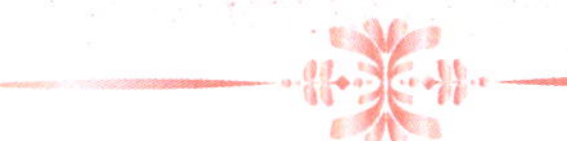

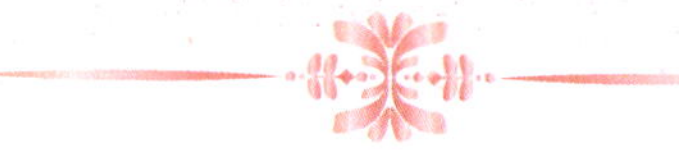

DEAR DAUGHTER,

"ONCE YOU EMBRACE YOUR VALUE, TALENTS AND STRENGTHS, IT NEUTRALIZES WHEN OTHERS THINK LESS OF YOU."

— ROB LIANO

FROM FRIENDS AND LOVED ONES

Daughter, you are surrounded by love. The following pages are letters from some family and friends who will always be an integral part of your journey.

REMINDER

"ANYONE WHO DOES ANYTHING TO HELP A CHILD IN HER LIFE IS A HERO TO ME."

— *inspired by Fred Rogers*

QUOTE

IT TAKES A VILLAGE TO RAISE A CHILD

An African Proverb

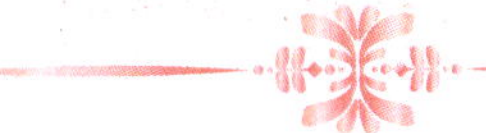

A list of Books to Enrich Your Mind

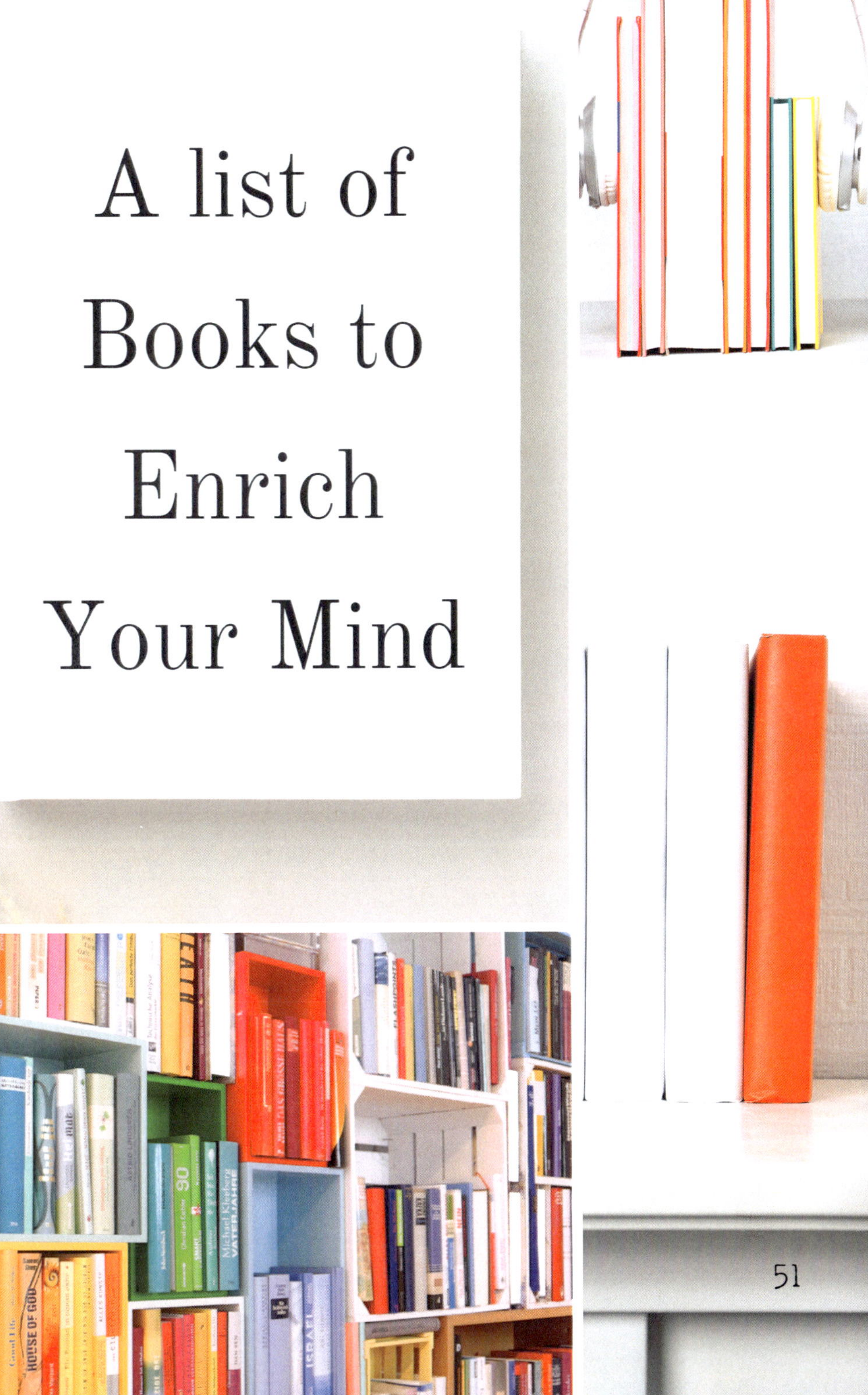

"BOOKS GIVE A SOUL TO THE UNIVERSE, WINGS TO THE MIND, FLIGHT TO THE IMAGINATION, AND LIFE TO EVERYTHING."

— *Attributed to Plato*

RECOMMENDED READING LIST

Title

Author

Title

Author

Title

Author

Title

Author

Title

Author

Title

Author

Title

Author

Title

Author

Title

Author

RECOMMENDED READING LIST

Title
Author

Title
Author

Title
Author

Title
Author

Title
Author

Title
Author

Title
Author

Title
Author

Title
Author

"YOU MAY NOT CONTROL ALL THE EVENTS THAT HAPPEN TO YOU, BUT YOU CAN DECIDE NOT TO BE REDUCED BY THEM."

— *Maya Angelou,*

PHOTOS

PHOTOS

JOURNAL

PAGES FOR MY
DAUGHTER'S THOUGHTS

"IF DAUGHTERS REFLECT ON THEIR DAYS, THEY WILL BECOME BETTER AT RECOGNIZING AND CREATING POSSIBILITIES IN LIFE."

Inspired by Trevor Carss

How are you feeling today?

Things you are *grateful* for :

1.

2.

3.

Today's affirmations :

My mood today is...

Calm	Rested	Creative
Happy	Angry	Sad
Anxious	Playful	Grateful

My daughter's thoughts

How are you
feeling today?

Things you are
grateful for :

1.

2.

3.

Today's
affirmations :

My mood today is...

Calm	Rested	Creative
Happy	Angry	Sad
Anxious	Playful	Grateful

My daughter's thoughts

How are you
feeling today?

Things you are
grateful for :

1.

2.

3.

Today's
affirmations :

My mood today is...

- Calm
- Rested
- Creative
- Happy
- Angry
- Sad
- Anxious
- Playful
- ________

My daughter's thoughts

How are you *feeling* today?

Things you are *grateful* for :

1.

2.

3.

Today's affirmations :

My mood today is...

Calm	Rested	Creative
Happy	Angry	Sad
Anxious	Playful	Grateful

My daughter's thoughts

How are you
feeling today?

Things you are
grateful for :

1.

2.

3.

Today's
affirmations :

My mood today is...

Calm	Rested	Creative
Happy	Angry	Sad
Anxious	Playful	Grateful

My daughter's thoughts

How are you *feeling* today?

Things you are *grateful* for :

1.

2.

3.

Today's affirmations :

My mood today is...

Calm	Rested	Creative
Happy	Angry	Sad
Anxious	Playful	Grateful

My daughter's thoughts

How are you
feeling today?

Things you are
grateful for :

1.

2.

3.

Today's
affirmations :

My mood today is...

Calm	Rested	Creative
Happy	Grateful	Playful
Anxious	Sad	Angry

My daughter's thoughts

How are you *feeling* today?

Things you are *grateful* for :

1.

2.

3.

Today's affirmations :

My mood today is...

Calm	Rested	Creative
Happy	Grateful	Playful
Anxious	Sad	Angry

My daughter's thoughts

How are you *feeling* today?

Things you are *grateful* for :

1.

2.

3.

Today's affirmations :

My mood today is...

Calm	Rested	Creative
Happy	Grateful	Playful
Anxious	Sad	Angry

My daughter's thoughts

A Daughter's Affirmation

by

Achieng Oreta

I am the daughter,
who is ever filled with divine wisdom.
My frequency is joy and abundance,
I am powered by love.
My path is consistently safe,
I continuously make wise decisions.
I am present, beautiful, healthy, and
successful.
I consistently rise and follow the enlightened
path.

i love you.

DESIGNED BY ACHIENG ORETA

First hardcover edition December 2022.

Printed in the USA.

www.ingramcontent.com/pod-product-compliance
Lightning Source LLC
Chambersburg PA
CBRC091645100726
47973CB00019B/244

* 9 7 9 8 3 3 0 2 3 1 6 7 6 *